THE MEN

THE MEN

A LYRIC BOOK

LISA ROBERTSON

Book*hug Press
Toronto 2022

FIRST EDITION, THIRD PRINTING
© 2006, 2022 by Lisa Robertson

The production of this book was made possible
through the generous assistance of the Canada
Council for the Arts and the Ontario Arts Council.

 **Canada Council
for the Arts**   **Conseil des Arts
du Canada**

 **ONTARIO ARTS COUNCIL
CONSEIL DES ARTS DE L'ONTARIO**
an Ontario government agency
un organisme du gouvernement de l'Ontario

LIBRARY AND ARCHIVES CANADA
CATALOGUING IN PUBLICATION

Robertson, Lisa, 1961–
The men : a lyric book / Lisa Robertson

Poems.

ISBN 0-973974257
1. Title

PS8585.03217M45 2006   C822'54
C2006-901972-X

PRINTED IN CANADA

for Erin O'Brien

MEN DEFT MEN

Men deft men mental men of loving men all men
Vile men virtuous men same men from which men
Sweet and men of mercy men such making men said
Has each man that sees it
Cry as men to the men sensate
Conceptual recognition the men
And their poverty speaking to the men
Is about timeliness men is about
Previous palpability from which
The problematic politics adorable
And humble especially
Young men of sheepish privilege becoming
Sweet new style

Each man – I could write
His poem. He needs no voice.
But what would I take from it. Our facades are so
Minor. What would I begin to say
If his words were
My poem. I am preoccupied with grace
And have started to speak expensively – as in
Have joys
Which look like choice
Ill-matched to its consequence
As laughter to a fall – bad memory
Poorly researched life
The men's
Cocks
And their faces
As we do so
Fall upwards.

Men, I'm 39 and my poem
A purple scarf
Of men
From which men move
Men sweet and smooth
Men auditorily ignored
Men by virtue of men
Following men
Make me tremble.

What we refer to as men is any
Communication we begin to perpetrate
A priori for this man the men
Want less and no less than the
Holding and thus a spree
Of men.

I address men
And their faces
And no shame

From sweet mercy each man makes deft wounds makes
women and disquietude and something from what
I am. What is it to open upwards towards the men
hospitably to make something factless from the spurious
craving for men from most delicate improbable men
from amourous spiritual men from the education of the
emotions of men devotedly from whom I cannot remain
indifferent as men.

Men, I'm sad I must die.
These are beautiful shores.

Sensate conceptual recognition the men
And their poverty speaking
Language this theoretical
Clatter the pigeons on the ridgepole fluff
And fuck and fly off

The funny pathos of men – I salute this.

As for the men, we did toss our declinations and
    conjugations to and fro as they do who by way of
    a certain game
Of men
Conjugate men.
What I saw, I saw perfectly.
For amongst other things
I could neither mingle nor confound
I could neither reduce this exquisite toil nor teach
But I could entertain
As pure as a latin tongue
As pure
As two of my countrymen
Tractable and yielding
Upon a dark damask
I love it exceedingly and I satisfy my judgement.

Clear and regular the men being more and more
exasperated would go to the shops. The value of the
money is changed according to the men who repeat
virtue and truth, virtue and truth and things written on
coins accordingly.

The men change limited constructs into easy patterns.
They determine on it. They point to the picture and
they nurture their hearts. They find time to analyze
conditions frequently. Men's commands are laminated
by other methods – at the end of his frontiers there is
left a free, indifferent and neutral space which is the
sexuality of the men and they suffer. They commonly
harbour their father's bodies in themselves and in their
marrow.

The men have divers lusters heady with vibration
    whence their opinion
Men, I am shady and terrestrial.

I have a friend who knew
Debord – the men are pleased
And their faces open
Sexually. There is no concrete
Or eternal thing there.
We form attachments. And then we
Go visiting. I do not mind. I
Go too. I saunter
Somewhere. The quick
Brown fox jumps
Over the lazy dog speaking
Language.

Sweet new style
I walk as appearing
Everything became what I saw.
I pour into the style
Of the manikin
And moisturize
I pour into
The men. I've been
Changed
By men
You don't know
Excellently
I am home.

The men carrying his thoughts beyond his school
beyond all experience beyond idealism the men beyond.
I see it everywhere. Their immanent use will not damage
me. My place is grasped by my auditor. Their work is a
textbook. Without finding the world sufficient they give
it some liberty. To consider the power and domination
these bodies have I suckle them. There is not a man
alone there is not sufficiency nor geometry but there is
beauty and greatness and thirst.

The
Men are enjambed.

The men find themselves happy only insofar
As they gratify an inclination.
They are men of warmth and humour and
Acute sensitivity and if I choose
To speak of them it is no trifle.

To speak of the men is no trifle.

They are both sublime and
Beautiful, delicate
And copious, rolling and touching
And rubbing one against another
In their most serious actions
But nothing makes them men
But their word in the new-found world.
I study them more than any other subject
Studying hard in this disordered rabble
Remembering to drink water
Judging soundly like a man
The ceremonies and decorations
The opportunities for ornament
Inorganic and misty they exist
Against gravity and they fail
Glamorously their ideal which is to float
In the air without any support
So beautiful and sucking.

Let the thought here be planted
That the men want to float
Just the pink tip of their
Thing touching the firmament.

Whence men that achieve both
Clarity and embellishment, sur-embroidered
With clandestine emotion
Goya painted their eyes
Into women
Thus
The psychic life
Of pigment.

The men used to dream about the future and they
   dreamt this.

It is love
They announce
The men
Flow down
The pen
And they write.
They have only
The reticence
Of intimacy.

You really love
The men.
We do.

The men have a house
Of rooms and time
To walk through them
Pondering their sons
And daughters, feeling
Loss and the long tiredness
Of passing. At such times
In exhaustion
They show you the liner notes. Look
Say the men, look
And the first webs of lust
Flicker
Near the window
And their shirts are sweet
And their sweat bitter:
Just delicious.

This may be ventured –
The morning of the men
Singly and steadily
Light and livid
Loveliest and most loveable
Ditto the men
A glow of larch.

As daintily as candle-lights the men
Rise from civil business to
Theological truth and the wooing
Of it, clear and serene. Nature
Is weak; the men feel pain
They fear death. Their limbs
Are not the quickest. Thereby
Imagine what the
Men are, groaning
And convulsing.
We are weary in the watching.
I am.

The new men sung and the weeping of the men
At break of day is echoed in the valleys
The man whose face flows down
More than the other men, men of no
Failings vanishing through the dawn
Where did the men get the gold
So extraordinarily
Leaving little of me left
And from what men
(The men that burn in my heart)
I should escape. I am ashamed.
If the men turn towards me
Where are the rights of my solitude?

All men these days would like to wear
Grief and noise. All men
Seem to think. In their eyes
Remains that live burden.
I suffer equally. Brief
Wrath of the men
Is very long as if
The men had intellect
And wings and people's
Voices. The men
Exist
Against gravity and they fail. They form
Precisely and in great
Density
Too much information.
The men are fragile and finite
Involuntary the men
Nuzzling
The streets of the centuries
The women's names in them
Moving the women's thighs
Directly.

Perhaps this is the fantasy
Of men. Their house
Like sunlight
Before delving. Girls
In our dresses
Print dresses in memory. The light
Dripping and producing
Freedom
Sexually.

I've sexually seen the opacity of men.
I feel modest about it.

The whole prehistory of the water
Is about timeliness men is about
Previous palpability from which
Among a grove of ilex
The problematic politics adorable
Young men of sheepish privilege becoming
Less adorable I thought words and forgot
Them.

The men beneath the green I saw
Until there have been men
Like these alone or in the world
And blazing men as years
The men close my eyes as those
That melt me going.
I fear life will change before
The men or even regain
Yourself, the men heavens made
Just so. Culpable.
Where did you get the gold
Glow of larch
Leaving little?

I've touched the men who stopped
My tongue, I've touched the men
In the free breeze foreignly. But this
Immaculate equal
Grows as I speak
And their two styles flossy.
And their two
Styles flossy.
And hence experience
Analogy.
But only in relation
To the men
And my own eyes.

In this rough verse
Unavoidably the men
All bordered with sky blue
Stand alone
And my little bed also
Bearing nothing more.
I have only the reticence of intimacy.

EVENING LIT THE GNAT

Evening lit the gnat uncommonly.
What is left for me to undertake?
Our passion to speech in the syllable of the name a
    transparency
In the transparency a gland
Which is solid
And scary.
Trashy sweet brain I give it to them
In dry air and summer light.

A man could learn a lot from a conchologist – a man
Could learn amazement.
Large free animals
With heads of dogs
Eject form.
The men emerge indolently
Like last human things like names.

Trashy sweet brain adoring and adoring them.
Amazement ejecting form like a gland, trashy.
To speech in the middle of dry transparency.
Its juice there indolent.

Head of a dog, I speak to you now.
Head of a boy I speak out of your mouth into that olden
    sweet green
It is for me now to undertake
Last human things.

This is where I speak from the juicy mouth of a man or
boy devotedly saying I am, I am, and it is a song. This is
where I tear the cloth. This is where the word falls out
in the form of a dog, a black dog, a dog that seems to
speak, and what the dog says is poverty is sap. So I lick
it up sweetly. Now what do they want. What's sucked
is hydromel and I lick them as they smoke and these
are syllables these are last things plunging and my brain
adores the form of the world with a decorous amplitude.
This is poverty and it's as false as the poem.

False juicy mouth say anything. Entirely synthetically I
speak to them because everything is poverty and we call
this hydromel.

Hydromel in wildness and hydromel in the form of the
world and hydromel dripping from the face, your face,
the face of the men, hydromel filling the boats in the
interminable night. Sucking hydromel. Call it style or
call it what we do, it's poverty. Because unreasonably
I adore them I utter this word hydromel, I'm for it,
it's what I do. Hydromel violet hydromel cadmium
hydromel apples I am
Ejecting form
For their face.
It's for me now to undertake this thing. I have called it
men and now I call it hydromel.

I call out hydromel to the men I take all of their style
and I turn it to poverty. Who can say which loses? I call

out hydromel to the ladies as false as the gorgeous poem.
This is referential stability. This is our passion to speech.
Hydromel in the meadows and in the evening light
especially. I have plenty so I give it to them false human
face men fluttering men recumbent men married men in
cognition lady's men men homosexual men of the true
synthetic space men as glamorous as dew. Your name is
a syllable on my face and I speak it from your own juice.
What's prior to cognition. Amazed head of a man I feed
you violets and fall upwards bleating.

If in the warm day each thing expanded to the form of
its word, if weather were poverty and I Laura never died,
if I Hazel never wept, if I understood the sentences in
the form of the world, if all the falsity remained internal
to beauty, my juicy mouth would want to say just
these things as the trees opened and to them. Entirely
synthetically I speak in air with their choice of good
words. Some things result from thought and yet they are
not contingent. I refer to the idea of Spring and I refer
to poverty. Humanly they are architectures especially
in the evening light. They have undone us and they are
not aesthetical. We have thought them before Laura ever
died, undertaking to fill the boats. I have called it The
Men, passing the vanished barbershops, and the cabs
empty, and the soiled caps cast on the street, my coins in
my hard fist reading Truth. Nostalgia isn't cognition. As
much falsity as I can use, I carry. The men shimmer.

Prior and excellent head of the boy
Speaking words tell me the history of
The face. Tell me where it exits
Faceless and slipping from
Structure. I'm ready to believe
When speech slips out of the animal's head
It seems normal. I know the spot
On the skull where it exits and I rub it.

By means of concepts they pretended
Language and the moderation of extravagance
To satisfy the conditions of the fabulous problem
And the concepts that supply them with matter
Such as the experience of the lily behind me
Which nearly spoke
Or clearly called to me in its lily way.
This is a speculative song.
I hope to advance further.
It is the most difficult task I have undertaken.

By means of the construction of concepts
We shall not discover men in the concept
In my intuition no man belongs in the concept
Of necessity. Obscurely the men are preamble
My concatenation admits each flesh
In its silky conceptual covering
Thus the acute men produce themselves
In fully the era of my adolescence.
Trashfuck or hydromel:

How do I make them actual?
I stand or fall with the solution
And the thickness of the lives I stand on
Or this is all in vain – thus
Their transcendental problem.

Now, prior and excellent head of the boy
Faceless and slipping from
Structure and encumbered
With acts I summarize. By means of the concepts you
    pretended
To satisfy the conditions of the fabulous problem
Which nearly spoke.
I hope to advance further, devotedly
Prolix
Out in your clear prose.

We shall not discover men in the concept
Nor in the calls on the stair
In my intuition no man belongs in the concept
With his remorse
Ordinarily the men are preamble
Trashfuck or hydromel.

As for the rubbery mastery and enchantment and linkage
When I have required a man to submit
I have regretted the decision.

A mental attitude
To my general puzzlement
Expands regardless of satisfaction.
With such violence
I greet
The transcendent
I lay at the foundations of cognition and wait to achieve
    my number
I wait to achieve my bundle
I wait to achieve their
Doubt.
They are the forms of our sensibility
And the texture of their eagerness is a system
And my despair is not a problem
It is under my breastbone and speaks
In the smell of planks and silence.

They have an electric fan
And the rubbery mastery
Of transcendence.

A RECORD

I'm making a record of the men as I know them, their
hours and their currencies and their simple sex. I'll be
their glamorous thing and then I won't. Their coats are
casual, they are entirely casual in their stance and I paste
my record up.

When a man rides with a demon, when he transmits and
snags, when a man feels his psyche work all over america
in its humble way, when he has no obligation, when
he marches on, when a man marches on, when he has
hideous knowledge and he marches with it in the burnt
grass, when men believed so many things, when a man's
name is sewn in the label of my coat, when the men's
cocks face out to sea, lovely

And I thank them.

Under any meridian I was born
In the climate of them, all bordered in blue
Men in the same level, three or four men together, one
Man placed by himself, ranked, his good
Points primitive, each having a liberty, each
Having a frailty to purchase.

There is a physiognomy of men, an
Inscription upon all his works
The inscription of their several forms, constitutions, parts
And operations. I dare not call at random
I dare not verify their prognostics.
Their notation is landscape. I cannot verify it.
The common wonder of all men in the fabric of one man
Is it happiness or misfortune?
There was never anything so like another.
I cannot condemn a man for ignorance
I cannot condemn the men. Their reason wears me.
I envy no man, instruct no man, nor
Condemn a man. Scholars are men.
These are the men that must step out
From the visionary landscape.

No man can censure
No man can judge
No man knows.
Yet is every man observed by any man.
I perceive every man.
There is no man that apprehends and no
Man that so nearly apprehends.
To multiply in men
God loves man
Thus one man cuts through another with a clean edge.
It is like a man, this one fabric
Of man. But men's minds also find no rest. With all men
There is no man alone because every man is the world.
Men that look
Sometimes do speak. Every man truly
Positions men. Decadently I withdraw their landscape.
Thus I perceive a man. The twelfth part of man is the
    crooked piece of man.
I find no rest in any
Thereby becoming the unstable element.
In brief, I am content.

From a dream and the conformity to law
Apart from my thoughts
They rouse from their organic slumber
To present themselves to my senses
With their even gaze.
I have nothing left for them but the absolute tiredness of
    the series.
I speak of men as they appear to me
Not of men in themselves
I have only experience
And no knowledge.

In experience and for experience only
For the sake of experience they are men.
They have substance for experience only.
I distinguish them from a dream.
This is therefore a decisive experiment.
I know more than this but I can't reach it
And real pain crowds my real head
In the representation.
Their earth is so little
We cannot attribute freedom to the men.

Awful sighs that never end I venture from my style
Against style
As birds, grass, evening
Temporarily boy-like
To make the thing intelligible.
The same actions are free
That caption
Determination
Such as awful sighs that never end
In cinema
In fact
This is all I require –
That in the literal transparency
I see the dark of evening
I see the night of the green woods tomorrow
I see animate and waiting a rich shore
That's neither love nor notes, freedom nor reason, story
    nor lyric, boredom nor strings,
Albertine.

OF THE VOCABLE

At times the sound of the vocable is
The vocable of the men. It sits, it
Emits, it leaves the solemn limit
Beneath a tent of lilac
I want a simple book too, I want those
Fabulous testimonies in the style
Of toile de jouy, I want them to bestir
Themselves
For the duration of a diminutive
To inhabit this voice:

The sidewalks in light are the sidewalks of childhood
with the men walking on them past the trees of
childhood also and the sky flattened with light as in
the childhood of the men. Memory stands up in slow
motion and moves in their light. Being the men involves
knowing.

I speak to them now in all my categories.

Men, we are already people.

My idealism concerns them. Transcendental or better in the second landscape I whelp them. Hence they can never be omitted. All landscape is second. They are indigenous and mute. Ordinarily they emote in their bare hotel, ordinary and unavoidable, or in my sensuous intuition. I, on the contrary, say, in order to avoid all idealism, my despair is not a problem.

In actuality the men are superadded. The concept of the men is elastic. To have been forgiven by them is delicious and tawdry. We should not forget this fact.

Inside the men are people. They have a small dreamy
    heart. Sometimes I am immobilized by sadness as
    the night enters their window.

Both things perceive: the men and inside them the
    people. Nothing originates that does not come
    through their window. When through the thickness
I see the tilting
I do not see it
In the syrupy and shimmering element
I do not see it
In the recurrent subject
My cool pleasure expanding coolly
To my general puzzlement.

Plentifully of reason, plentifully
Of ceremony, plentifully the pastoral of the men in the
    middlediction that they
Have. The men in their short-sleeved shirts
Are glad
Beautious and goodly
With beauty and tallness
And a kind of fear
And sweet glance plentifully
The men breathe into me, tender, phallic, kimonoed,
    and I, in the middle of my life, reply
That I would like to very much
In this brief season
I can't tell you what it's like to be in the rooms with
    them, the
Nothingness entwined with the mental and the odour of
    smoke
From the hallway.
I'm wearing this silky thing for
My skin and the men plentifully
And I am so sad.

The men are as mysterious as art, as
Glamorous as dew and
Plentifully
Their faces
Fall upwards.

Miles away and
Some
Years ago

Silvery and half-erased by a morning-like desire, and the
cabs empty, the men live on air, like an orchid, and on
their choice of good words.

In their evening peregrinations the men have invented a mirror that remembers repeatedly. They are flying more and more deeply into what men are with their little wings. As the afternoon becomes evening they, composing the sullen sky, the clear faces of their mothers in memory, break up like weather. They break up like weather.

Tarnished river, streets serpentine, sulphur lights, black massing of foliage, papaya slice of sky, it's 6:45 and I'm 39.

Lawyerly the men walk through impartial stripes of
light and repeat the incredible number. There is always
a theme. To breathe the common air of the men, to fall
where they fall, cry clearer than any bell, to coil and
thrust and seek

The young men in ads this spring, men in TV, I glimpse
the little teeth in their passion. Equivalent, dwindling.
Honestly, I postpone them.

They cannot resist their own honour.

Clearer than any bell
Their little eyes widen
I glimpse the little teeth
In their passion the men very eagerly
To catch new light
In general terms
Retire illuminated.
Such is the potent harmony.

What they are now in general terms.

Astonished, weakened, nuzzling. The men are as heavy
as smoke. I glance through them. It would be silent,
puddled up, alone in space and unfabulous. Casually
frothing they demand a proportion. Instead of seeking
the cause of the men, the cool plunging into them,
the labour of the men like foam, I supply the surface
with men. By this procedure men gain. Propositions
constitute the subject of men, gathered up by some like
foam. To evade it is impossible. The museums will leave
traces in them. The men will overflow. Red, yellow,
green-silver, maroon, blue, black are the men and stuck
in the streak, the twist, the line, like paint. It will appeal
to me always. But men ran his ship ashore

There to let it lie. Thus the postponement.
I'm 39.

TRUE SPEECH

With constancy and languor and a simple face
To find what is constant
I write
In the bonny day of them
With equal acuteness and clearness
In the bonny day of them
Among these various attitudes
I never sigh, I never sigh
At volition
Nor the little leaves opening
What's loved and known is hydromel
The rest, prudence.

This is my first true speech.

Their cabins smelling of cedar, roughness of red blankets, splinters of music – this is incorrect because it sounds like a movie. But the men were ordinarily sexual, little else. What I'm feeling is the seizure of language in newness then, the absolute strangeness of their kind, fascination and terror and humility and the internal restfulness. Everything I can remember about summer is the men.

There were a thousand and twenty-two stars and fear and lust moving together like make-up over all the cities of them, their spines laid back in the seizure of strangeness. There were burnt-out skies of flat and leaf-laden nature, the rough territories of their hands floating over the surface of our ragged breath and their sadness built of doubt. Whether these ideas are true or false they are certain. Everything I can remember about summer is the men, portraits, still-lifes, the stiff leaf of the camelia. The men became what they are like rather than what they are –

A lyric
Comportment
With succulence and bigness of deep red.

How boring and fascinating the men.
I do this for them with structure and bigness.

I want to speak about their sentiment as a secular event.
The weather is as it looks, framed in nostalgia and
money. The fall of the light is the fall of the secular. The
men are a house inside out. They are ten men

Named Phil and Jeff
In September.

They elaborate a cogitation. In this way I arrive at the thought of them. Increasingly their oxygen is my own and I in my little coloured shoes to please them. Their revolution is permanent and mine a decoration. When the trees smear their sky, when their poems are the periphery of the West, when they swim from their silver docks, I swim too and we communicate in water. This was September, there were three of us, and one was a man. I feel passionately about their gardens.

Each of us psycho-sexually is a man, dreaming and convulsing, plunged into some false Africa manically like a poet. The leaves are turning pink, or they are thickening and sturdy. Why go on changing? I like garlands and green clothes and my face is simple. I know their soul is pain and it doesn't help me. I have experienced each of them, and the calls on the stairs. I go with them to a point.

The weather is normal. I lay my ear against the curved-downward ceiling to hear the rain. The men are a ceiling, and their heart outside. Here it would be suitable to speak of the men and money.

Surely I could, like a poet of some previous epoque,
    praise them
In some sparse rhyme
And with humble touches.
The paint is thin, the light
Breaks through their skin
With precision and ardour
Or more properly refracts
Rather than absorbs this praise
And with humble touches
They are happiest
In stillness and their silver smoke drawn pretty.

To feel, to laugh, to ride horses
Is what the men are for.

Noble men fair men men glowing with
Their names men of the world's
Four parts men who sigh
Trilustral avid men men breathing

Some have gone to buy food
And some are returning and some
Never do. Some will die
Among books and I'm tired
Of the school of errors. Some
Put me in darkness. And some
Transparently slender in summer
Are so bold, though dulcet shade
Is brief, and some moan
As I enter the night on its hinge.
Some smoke as you lick them. Some
So dull, some equivalent, some
Dwindling. It's late, rivers and acorns
And I'm tired. Some's desire
Is not my desire, and some's
Desire dulcet by my estimate. But
There are diverse and new
Things in any climate. Some
Think poverty is sap for a poet
And some will always seek
Other love, other leaf, other light.
Some avoid indolence and some say
"I can't live because I used to live"
I won't give them the formula.
In friendship and the thin air
Some speak the word hydromel
And I repeat them. The dulcet shade
Is brief my men

And this is my first true speech
And this with a decorous amplitude
And this in the middle of my life, the
Streets silent and the night all covered in questions
And this desire which discerns
Is my desire
And this ornament
Is my ornament

In this history there are instruments
Like faces of men rough and inaccurate
There are terrestrial decorations
Called human there are propositions
Complex and deciduous and sticky

But I believe that their right
Shoulder recedes and their left leg comes forward
Powerfully, that always they are
Accompanied by experiments
Like putti, I believe that the men at
The parking meter, the men in the
Tunnel, the men near the unopen fence
Romantic with skies the men naturally
Playing
Won't change my life by speaking

Ah
The lovely face of them
Their window all mixed up with concepts
And their lovely forest a concept
Their window is a life
The trees outside
Their window are another
Life where I'd endure but

The entire tradition speaks against this.

Subtle men
Men mental
Men of love
Gentle

Spirit tossed
Visual spirits
With spirituality of trembling
That makes them humble

Any specific man moves
His sweet soft spirit
Beneath Wednesday's umbrella

The spiritual men are poor.
Though it pours from their eyes
Their strength empties itself.
I spoke in their voices.

I wished simply to represent them.
One man reaches out his arms.
The wind is strong.
The street bends slightly.
The horizon vanishes.

(In Vancouver as the dark winter tapered into spring
I undertook to sing
My life my body these words
The men from a perspective.

For all those who confuse
Flirtation with monogamy
I drain the golden glass

They exit and glance upwards
Adjust their little caps)

ACKNOWLEDGEMENTS

to the editors of the magazines that published earlier versions of some poems: *Raddle Moon, Matrix, Tessera* and *Upstairs at Duroc*.

to the Canada Council for the Arts, for an arts grant that helped support the writing of this book.

to Erin O'Brien and Lucy Hogg, two painters whose portraits of men first spurred these poems.

ALSO BY LISA ROBERTSON

The Apothecary
XEclogue
Debbie: An Epic
The Weather
Occasional Works and Seven Walks from the Office for
    Soft Architecture
Rousseau's Boat

COLOPHON

Manufactured in an edition of 2000 copies
in the spring of 2006 by Book*hug Press.
Second printing, summer 2014.
Third printing, fall 2023.

Type + Design by Jay Millar

Printed in Canada

bookhugpress.ca